God Created

T. REX

"In the beginning God created..." Genesis 1:1

God Created *T. rex*

by Christy Hardy and Lori Fausak

First printing: July 2022

ISBN: 978-1-946246-99-8

Please visit our website for other books and resources: ICR.org

Printed in the United States of America.

God Created

T. REX

ICR
INSTITUTE
FOR CREATION
RESEARCH

Dallas, TX
ICR.org

Christy Hardy and Lori Fausak

TALK ABOUT T. REX

It's easy to spot a *Tyrannosaurus rex*! See the upright posture, huge head, tiny arms, and long, heavy tail? But you won't find a live one today. *T. rex* was a theropod dinosaur that walked on Earth just thousands of years ago. We keep discovering more about this famous dino as new fossils and traces of its existence are uncovered.

DID YOU KNOW?

God designed theropods like *T. rex*, *Deinonychus,* and *Spinosaurus* to have mostly hollow bones. This made their skeletons lighter for speedy racing and chasing.

Deinonychus

4

Spinosaurus

T. REX WAS CREATED

The Lord Jesus created the world and everything in it in six days. On the sixth day, He created land animals and the first humans, Adam and Eve. Among those land beasts was the mighty *T. rex*. On that day, God said that everything He had made was "very good."

Could a ferocious creature like *T. rex* really be "very good"? Well, Jesus created all animals at that time, including *T. rex*, to eat plants. It wasn't until Adam and Eve sinned that the world became cursed and animals began to attack people and each other. Death was not a part of God's original very good creation.

SIX DAYS OF CREATION

DAY 1

DAY 2

DAY 3

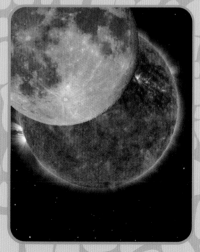

DAY 4

DAY 5

DAY 6

NAME THAT DINO

Tyrannosaurus is Greek for "tyrant lizard." And *rex* is Latin for "king." When taken together, *Tyrannosaurus rex* means "king of the tyrant lizards."

Who named the *T. rex*? Henry Fairfield Osborn, the president of the American Museum of Natural History, came up with the name in 1905. He said *T. rex* was "the most ferocious dinosaur to walk the earth!"

DID YOU KNOW?

The word dinosaur wasn't invented until 1841. So, legends about reptile creatures called "dragons" may be based on people's real encounters with dinosaurs in the past.

Henry Fairfield Osborn (right).
Drawing of a *Tyrannosaurus* skeleton by
William D. Matthew that was published with
Osborn's *T. rex* paper in 1905 (below).

SCAVENGER OR HUNTER?

Scientists have disagreed over whether *T. rex* was a scavenger or hunted live prey. Scavengers such as buzzards and coyotes eat things that are already dead. Did *T. rex* do this? Like detectives, scientists can only examine clues to understand what happened in the past.

At first they thought *T. rex* wasn't able to chase down prey because its arms were so short. So, maybe it was a scavenger. But bite marks found on other dinosaurs clearly came from a *T. rex*. And *T. rex* needed a lot of food to fuel its large body. It would need to hunt to survive in today's fallen world. A younger, smaller *T. rex* could have survived by searching for dead meat.

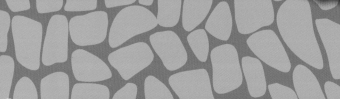

GROWING UP

T. rex most likely started out as a hatchling in a football-size egg. But we can't know that for sure. Why? Because scientists have never found a *T. rex* egg! Since other theropod dinosaurs hatched from eggs, it's likely that *T. rex* did, too. A newly hatched *T. rex* was probably about the same size as a chihuahua.

Young *T. rex* fossils have smaller and thinner heads, long legs, and blade-like teeth. The skeletons show that these *T. rex* teenagers could probably run faster than an adult, which had more muscle.

6 feet

12 feet

40 feet

A full-grown *T. rex* measured around 43 feet long and 12 feet high, and weighed about 7.5 tons. This is similar to the size and weight of a truck's semitrailer.

BUILT FOR STRENGTH

T. rex hunted with powerful legs and jaws. In fact, its teeth and jaw became strong enough to break through bone! Though *T. rex* was likely a ferocious predator, its battles were not easily won. Many *T. rex* fossils show broken bones, chipped teeth, or cracked skulls.

T. rex's arms were so short that it couldn't lift its prey to its mouth. But that doesn't mean those arms didn't pack a lot of muscle. The Lord Jesus gave *T. rex* great strength. Even those small arms could lift 400 pounds each! *T. rex* could have used the short arms and sharp claws to tear into prey, but no one can know that for sure.

T. rex tooth

The *T. rex* "Sue" had a rough life. Puncture wounds in her jaw were from a violent encounter with another *T. rex*. They healed, but she must have suffered from excruciating pain. Sue's femur, or thigh bone, had been broken. It naturally reset but could bear little weight. Similarly, several of her ribs had been broken. They also healed, but not completely. Sue recovered from this violent attack but suffered horribly for the rest of her life.

T. REX DID NOT EVOLVE INTO BIRDS

Most evolution scientists say that theropods like *T. rex* evolved into birds through small changes over time. But there are at least three problems with this idea.

1. Theropod dinosaurs have a different hip design than birds.

2. The fossil record doesn't show creatures that were part-dinosaur and part-bird. Every fossil found has either the design of a dinosaur or of a bird, but not both.

3. Dinosaurs and birds are found buried in the same rock layer. This means they lived at the same time.

What's the biggest problem of all? Evolution does not fit with what the Bible says. The book of Genesis tells us that God created every creature "according to its kind."

Dinosaurs have always been dinosaurs. And birds have always been birds.

Jesus designed birds with beaks to preen their feathers. Preening is vital to their survival. If dinosaurs had feathers, how could they preen them?

T. REX FOSSILS AND THE FLOOD

Most fossils formed during the Flood that's described in the Bible. God judged the evil world by covering it with water. He saved just one human family and two of every kind of land animal in a giant floating box called an ark. Everything outside the Ark was covered in layers of mud, which turned into rock. Plants and animals that were buried during the Flood became many of the fossils we find today.

Before the Flood, swampy land covered vast stretches of the earth. Animals grew larger, and the ground was filled with ferns and conifers. Open forests and a warm climate made everything lush, green, and full of life. *T. rex* would have thrived.

FOSSIL SUE

The *T. rex* fossil "Sue" stands peering over visitors at the Field Museum of Natural History in Chicago. Is the fossil called Sue male or female? No one knows for sure. And the name isn't a clue! Fossils are usually nicknamed after the person who found them.

Sue Hendrickson was on a trip in South Dakota when she discovered this fossil. She spotted some fossilized vertebrae of a dino spine sticking out of the side of a cliff. She started digging with her team of six people and ended up rescuing fossil Sue from the Flood rock.

Sue has given us a lot of information about what *T. rex* was like. In fact, other *T. rex* skeletons have been corrected thanks to Sue!

FOSSIL STAN

Meet Stan, the biggest *T. rex* fossil found so far. Stan is named after Stan Sacrison. He wasn't looking for fossils at all. Instead, he was looking at plant life when something on the cliffside caught his eye. Little did he know, it was the pelvis of a *T. rex*.

As a team dug up the fossil, they found two partly eaten dinosaurs nearby—an *Edmontosaurus* fossil and a *Triceratops* fossil! Could they have been Stan's last meal? We'll never know for sure. Stan has a complete skull, with all 58 teeth. It's the best *T. rex* skull ever recovered.

Edmontosaurus

Triceratops

FOSSIL SCOTTY

Scotty, at 30 years old, was like a battle-worn veteran. His fossil shows evidence of an infected jaw, impacted tooth, and broken ribs. And the wounds on his tail seem to be from the bite of another *T. rex*.

Even though most fossils are named after the scientist who found them, Scotty the *T. rex* was named after the drink the paleontologists shared in celebration of their find. They found him in Canada in the 1990s. The discovery started with a tooth and vertebra in 1991, and in 1994 they began digging up the rest of him. Overall, it took almost 10 years to completely uncover the fossilized skeleton.

FOSSIL BUCKY

Look, it's Bucky! This *T. rex* fossil, unlike the others talked about here, was only a teenager. Bucky is named after Bucky Derflinger, a young rancher and rodeo cowboy. Collecting fossils was a hobby for him ever since he was nine years old. He found this fossil when he was 20.

Bucky's bones were scattered all over. So, the dig site had to be huge, the size of a football field. But scientists are pretty sure they found every last bone left by Bucky.

FOSSIL "B-REX": MOR 1125

Bob Harmon discovered a *T. rex* in Iowa. It was nicknamed B-rex in his honor and is also called MOR 1125. Found in the year 2000, it's missing a lot of parts. But an amazing discovery was waiting in its bones.

Soft tissue was found in its femur. There were blood vessels, bone tissue, and even something like blood cells. This caused quite a stir! Why? Because soft tissue can't last one million years. It wastes away too quickly. A lot of scientists think this dinosaur was 68 million years old. But since they found real tissue inside, B-rex has to be much younger than they thought.

DID YOU KNOW?

Scientists have also found red blood cells in mosasaurs, hadrosaurs, turtles, and other fossils. These clues tell us dinosaur fossils are only thousands of years old, not millions.

JESUS, T. REX, AND THE NEW WORLD

Today, you might be thankful that there are no giant dinosaurs like *T. rex* roaming the earth. Or maybe you're sad that this awe-inspiring creature is extinct.

However you feel about it, know that one day God will set creation right. He has planned a day when the Lord Jesus Christ will return and animals will live in harmony with people again. He will make a new heaven and new earth! On that day, God will rule over all creation, and everyone who believes in Jesus will be one of His people. Are you ready for Jesus to come?

FIND OTHER CHILDREN'S RESOURCES AT
ICR.org/store

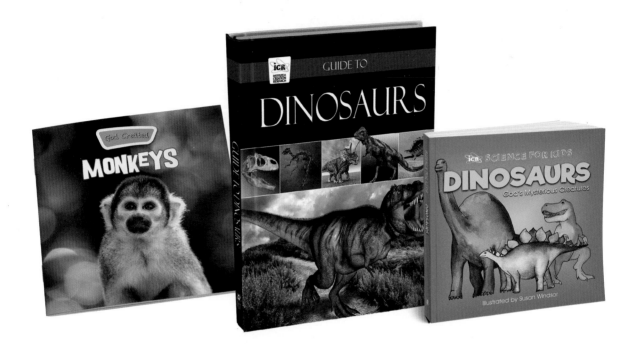